*i*Village
Solutions™

Best Advice on
FINDING MR. RIGHT

He is out there!

Real Women Share Their Secrets for
Getting & Keeping the Guy You Deserve

Foreword by KELLIE GOULD

RUTLEDGE HILL PRESS™

Nashville, Tennessee

A DIVISION OF THOMAS NELSON, INC.
www.ThomasNelson.com

Published by Rutledge Hill Press, a division of Thomas Nelson, Inc., P.O. Box 141000, Nashville, Tennessee 37214.

Library of Congress Cataloging-in-Publication Data

Best advice on finding Mr. Right / foreword by Kellie Gould.
  p. cm. — (iVillage Solutions)
Excerpts from online discussions on the iVillage.com web site.
  ISBN 1-4016-0042-5
  1. Mate selection. 2. Dating (Social customs) 3. Single Women.
I. Gould, Kellie. II. iVillage. III. Series.
  HQ801.B493 2003
  646.7'7—dc21   2002151017

Printed in the United States of America

03 04 05 06 07 — 5 4 3 2 1

CONTENTS

FOREWORD

By Kellie Gould

When I first met my husband, I thought, *Oh, he's not my type.* In fact, I almost didn't go out on a second date. (Okay, I almost didn't go out on a *first* date!) But a good friend—who had seen me through a lot of men I thought were *exactly* my type and turned out to be something altogether different—advised me to keep my head and heart open. Eight years later, I'm glad I did. The point is not that I met my Mr. Right, but that I *never would have* without the advice of my friend. And that's the value of this book: real advice from women who've been there.

Think of this book as a sit-down with your wisest girlfriends—the kind of women who will walk you through an embarrassing blind date and glorious first kiss—telling you what worked for them (and what didn't!).

The truth is, there's no one strategy that's right for everyone, and that's why I think you'll find *this* book so useful and inspiring. For every sticky issue ("Can I really date my cute coworker?"), you'll get tips from women with lived experience. It's like that friendly voice you wish you could hear in a moment of panic. ("What should I say when the guy at the gym finally notices me?") This book is not about following "rules" or "surrendering." It's about respecting yourself enough to find the man you really deserve.

Looking back on all the relationships I've navigated (some skillfully and others downright horribly), I realize that my best guides were women who had walked these paths before me. With this book, I share with you a new set of friends and some of the best advice I've ever heard for finding and keeping Mr. Right. But until you find him, just remember, as one wise woman says, "It's easy to feel like you have to be in a relationship because everyone seems to expect it. But if all you see are frogs, don't go jumping in the pond."

PREFACE

Since iVillage was founded in 1995, thousands of women have come to the discussion groups on the Website in search of advice about relationships. In dozens of groups devoted to the single life, they've found other women who gladly share their tips—with a big helping of friendship and support. In this book, you'll find the very best solutions women have shared with one another on iVillage.

iVillage would like to thank the members of iVillage.com's Relationships Channel (www.ivillage.com/relationships) for sharing their words of wisdom and inspiration. Without them, this book would not exist. We'd also like to thank the hundreds of community leaders who host our online discussion and support groups for the care, concern, and support they provide to our members. Suzanna Farlow and Rebecca Lockmiller Taylor provided invaluable assistance in helping us gather advice from the members of the iVillage community. And finally, many thanks to Kate Hanley for translating those many strains of online conversation into this book.

CHAPTER 1

Getting Your Head and Heart Ready

⌒

"What matters most is realizing that there is someone out there who would love to appreciate and share life with me—if only I'll let him."

FIGURING OUT WHAT YOU WANT

"I've been on several dates in the past few months. When I meet these guys, it seems like they are people I could really like. Then, after a few dates, I realize they aren't for me at all. How do I figure out exactly what I'm looking for in a boyfriend?" —M.P.

"You won't know who you are looking for until you know who you are. You will never find the right man if you are looking for him to complete you, to fill something that is missing, or to make you feel good about yourself. Be content enough with your life to feel special without a man at all. Then you will find someone who complements the woman you are."

"I have realized that I look for things in a mate that I have not cultivated in myself. For instance, I wanted an educated man, yet I never pursued my degree. Maybe that is why I always met such losers! Now that I am attending college again, the men I am meeting are either in school or have graduated."

"*I*n trying so hard to find the perfect relationship, maybe you just aren't giving the perfect relationship a chance to find you. I always thought that the kind of man I should be with was some successful Wall Street type. Meanwhile, the guy I married was a struggling freelance composer whom I only initially bothered with because he was interested in a script I was working on. I'd finally given up, and in giving up, there he was."

"Think about the types of men you've been choosing to date. I've had my share of players and, frankly, I'm done. Think about how they treat you, the little things they do. Look at men who treat others with respect. Ask yourself this: 'If I were dying of cancer tomorrow, would he be by my side or run for the hills?'"

"There's nothing wrong with going on two dates with someone and then realizing he's not for you. First of all, even if you think someone's nice, you can't tell if they're really for you after just one date. The other end of the spectrum is that you rely completely on first impressions—which is worse than spending a couple of evenings with someone who is perfectly nice but not for you."

LEARNING FROM YOUR OWN PAST RELATIONSHIPS

"I've always blamed the guy when things go sour. But now I have begun to accept that I share in the blame, too. How can I learn from my experiences and use them to find somebody who's good for me?" —D.W.

"The key to getting over old relationships is to look at them as learning experiences, and not failed attempts. You can take away knowledge from even a painful, emotional breakup about what you want and what you deserve, if you allow yourself to look at things that way."

"Figure out what it was that initially attracted you to the men you've been involved with. Then look at the issues that wound up ending the relationship. Be honest about yourself and about which of your qualities affected the relationship, as well. Then decide what sort of person you should be if you want to be involved with someone decent."

"I've learned that the only person who can make me happy is me. My advice: Put yourself first and do what you need to do. Don't sit back or put your partner's needs before your own. I've wasted too many years not realizing that and depending on a man to make me happy."

"Stop, look, and listen to what your intuition is telling you. The red flags start popping up pretty early on. It's important to pay attention to a person's actions and not their words. I have also learned that instant romance is not the way to go. Lasting relationships start out slowly and progressively grow. There has to be a good foundation to build on."

"My past relationships have taught me what love isn't: It is not mentally, physically, or verbally abusive; love doesn't make you cry or hurt; love isn't based on what-ifs or could-have-beens. Now I know what I had in the past isn't love and it awaits me in the future. I do not and will not fear love because of my prior experiences. They have enabled me to become wiser and made me realize what I am worth and what I want in a relationship."

Stop Sending Out Signals for Mr. Wrong

"I was stood up twice this week by two different guys. I am continually told that I am smart, sexy, fun, and generally good to be with, but lately I am a loser magnet!" —D.K.

" *If* you're just looking for someone to fill a void in your life, you will attract the wrong guys. You are sending out vibes that you don't really care about longevity or meaning. You just want someone to cure your loneliness. Your best bet: Start enjoying your own company. Then you will attract the right kinds of guys. "

" *Self*-confidence is the key. When you feel confident, you will stop wasting your time with guys who aren't right, because you will know you can do better. And your self-assurance will automatically attract more desirable, seemingly hard-to-get guys. "

"I always attract married men or men in serious relationships. It stumped me for the longest time. But now I think that when I meet someone who is technically unavailable, I am more comfortable around him and, thus, more attractive to him. I think that in order to start attracting available guys, the key is to take the pressure off the situation. Just because someone's single, I don't have to be interviewing him or putting on a show for him. It's not an audition."

"*I*t's easy to feel like you have to be in a relationship because everyone seems to expect it. It's very possible to be happy without a relationship or a man in your life. If you happen to meet someone great, so be it. If all you see are frogs, don't go jumping in the pond."

"*D*on't get hung up on looks. When you realize that good looks don't always mean a good personality, you will open yourself up to seeing good guys who don't necessarily turn heads wherever they go."

*B*OOSTING YOUR SELF-CONFIDENCE

"Men just don't seem to notice me. Guys seem to consider me as only a friend and not anything more. I don't want to go unnoticed anymore! How do I get better self-esteem and confidence?" —M.D.

"If you are unsure about yourself, your body language will indicate this. You're giving off signals that you want to be left alone. I know you can't help it, but it's because you don't feel worthy of anyone's attention. Remember that you're a vital, beautiful young woman and you need to find that within yourself. Stop looking for Mr. Right and look for Ms. I-Am-All-That-and-a-Bag-of-Chips— yourself!"

"*B*e true to yourself and someone will notice you. And when he does, he will be attracted to the real you, not some mirage."

"*Y*ou need to love yourself for all the good qualities you possess and then others will respond to that. The right man will love you regardless of how you look, as long as you accept yourself the way you are. Your attitude is what's important."

"Splurge on yourself. Take yourself shopping. Buy a crazy lipstick or wild eye shadow. Have makeup applied at the department store. A good makeup application makes me feel wonderful on days when I don't feel so good on the inside."

"When I wake up in the morning and get ready for work, I always tell myself, 'I am a confident person. I can do this with little or no problem.' And you know what? It works. If you tell yourself something over and over again on a daily basis, you'll begin to believe it. Then you'll project a sense of confidence that men will notice."

Making Room in Your Life for a Man

"At the moment I am just trying to figure out where I am in life. But in time I would really like to find a man. Where do I start?" —M.D.

"*L*et me share a little story with you: I saw a couple this morning. The guy reached for the girl's hand and they walked to the car together. At that moment, I realized that I was not open to having my hand held. I am standing in my own way of finding a good man by not allowing myself to believe he exists. Now I know that I need to work on believing that finding the right man is possible. If you start there, you'll find it possible, too."

"Clear the decks from past relationships or long strings of solitude by getting addicted to life. Take up a new hobby or an old one and do it. Schedule it regularly to keep you busy. Get rid of things your ex gave you that make you think of him. Rearrange your home. Move your furniture around. Start out your new life with a good cleanup."

"Take a vacation alone. I went to Club Med in the Caribbean and had a blast. I made friends on my own and it felt good to get away. No one knew that I had just gone through the breakup from hell. I got to try out new techniques for meeting men. If they didn't work, there were plenty of other men!"

"*I*t's a bit of a paradox. If you really want to make room for a man in your life, stop looking. If you're not on the hunt, you'll focus more on other interests and on being happy, which is much more attractive than calculated flirting. The tricky part is that you have to be emotionally open to the possibility of meeting someone great, without expecting it. "

"*I*f you hit it off with someone and want to make more room in your life to spend time with him specifically, great. But until that time, live your life to the fullest. Don't sit around with 'free nights' just in case some guy comes along to fill them up. "

CHAPTER 2

Meeting Men

~

"Don't be something you're not, just so you can attract a guy. You want someone who likes you for who you are, not for who you're pretending to be."

𝒲ORKING UP THE NERVE TO TALK TO A GUY

"It seems the guys I'm interested in either don't acknowledge my existence or go running in the opposite direction. I can't tell if my flirting isn't sufficient to let them know I'm interested, or if I'm being way too obvious. What is the best way to let a guy know you're interested in him, without coming on too strong?" —U.P.

"Men, like women, love to be complimented, just on different things: their jokes, their sense of fashion, and their intelligence. It's an ego boost when women come up to men and start talking. For example, ask a guy what time it is, then admire his watch. That usually starts a conversation. If you hit it off, it's okay to ask for his phone number, too. He'll know what you mean by asking; if he gives it to you, you'll know he's interested."

"If you're hanging out with a cluster of girlfriends, get away from them. Men fear a mob of women. Break away from your crowd for a moment to give the guy an opportunity to approach you. And if that doesn't work, spill your drink on him."

"Flirting does not have to be obvious or embarrassing. It can be as subtle as looking him in the eye while smiling, quickly brushing his arm, listening to him intently. But here is the hard part: You have to look him in the eye for several seconds, at least five or six seconds, while you have a friendly look on your face. He will get the idea and approach if interested."

"*If* you see someone at the gym who you think is cute, talk to him. For instance, say, 'Looks like we've got the same workout routine, don't we? By the way, my name's — —. What's yours?' You won't have done anything to embarrass yourself. You've just started a friendly conversation. If by some slim chance he does completely blow you off, he's the one who should be embarrassed because that's just plain rude."

"*My* tactic is to pick out the shy guy and talk to him. I introduce myself and start a light conversation. It's up to the guy to keep the conversation interesting to let me know he's interested. If he can't discuss a couple of different topics, then I politely exit. If it's going well, I work the conversation toward discussing an activity we both enjoy, to encourage him to ask me for a date."

$\mathscr{B}$EATING THE BAR SCENE BLUES

"I wonder if others find it difficult to meet nice guys. The bar scene doesn't ever seem to work out. Any suggestions on good ways to get involved in order to meet more people?"—H.A.

"*C*heck out a singles event, one that fits your personality as much as possible. For example, I attended a dating event because it was at a progressive spiritual church that offers yoga and meditation. This worked beautifully because all the men I met had spiritual interests."

"*S*tart by doing volunteer work. It's good for the soul — believe me — and you will meet normal people this way, men *and* women."

"*J*ust don't force yourself into doing something you're not interested in, such as joining a softball league if you're not into sports. I have found decent men to talk to at poetry workshops, coffeehouses, and bookstores."

"*I*'ve gone to many singles events, including Club Med four times. It always works out great. Carry yourself with confidence, and don't feel you have to talk a lot. If you end up sitting quietly in a group and just look like you're listening, that's sufficient."

"*I* think that meeting friends of friends is the best way. You have to encourage your friends to have dinner parties, barbecues, and other casual gatherings where you can get to know each other with no pressure. Also, you have to make a concerted effort to open up your social circle. You could easily meet a guy through a new girlfriend. Then your 'friends of friends' potential increases exponentially. "

Making Blind Dates Work

"Can you really meet someone worthwhile on a blind date? How do I make it work?" —R.T.

"*I*'ve been on a lot of blind dates and I think they're fun. First and foremost, be safe. Meet in a public place, take your own car, and arrange for a quick meeting. If you have fun meeting for a drink, there's no reason it can't turn into dinner and dancing, too."

"*B*e natural and pretend that you're meeting an old friend you haven't seen in a while. Ask questions—not prying or nosy, but friendly—and be interested in the answers. Hopefully you will be interested, but if not, no big loss."

"*Of* course blind dates can work: My sister met her husband that way, I met my current boyfriend that way, and my friend met his wife that way. You just have to have a good attitude, be laid-back, and just enjoy. I've been on dozens of blind dates in my life. Some were awesome, some very good, some mediocre, some icky, and only a few downright unpleasant."

" *B*lind dates can work if the person who introduces
the two of you has put some thought into the match-
making. But if you two have been set up just because
you're both single, don't get your hopes up. And
program your VCR. "

" *W*hatever you do, avoid the group setup, where a
group of your friends are going out and invite you both
along to see what happens. You both will end up sitting
there staring at each other, while everyone else looks at
you looking for the sparks. "

THE SKINNY ON ONLINE DATING

"I have a profile on an online dating site and have found some people I would like to write to, but I am not sure how the system works. Is it normal to exchange only a couple of emails or phone calls before meeting them?" —L.D.

"*O*nline dating sites are an excellent way to meet men. The main advantages are that all the men there are actually interested in dating someone, you can choose to talk to only men whose interests you share, and you get lots of time to talk to each man one-on-one."

"*I* talk with a guy via a few emails to see if there is even a reason to talk on the phone. After a few good phone conversations, I go ahead and meet him. Going too long without meeting in person causes problems. You create a bond in your mind that's based almost entirely on a fantasy."

"There's nothing better than emailing back and forth with someone only to find out they live around the corner from you. That's how I met the guy I am dating now."

"As a single mom with five kids under the age of 13, I don't have time to go anywhere to meet guys and don't drink, so bars are out. I have regularly corresponded with a few men via an online dating service. Whether or not I meet the man of my dreams, I am happy that I have made new friends. It has provided me with an outlet for adult conversation that I wouldn't have had otherwise."

"My sister met her husband online, and he is a great guy. She had been after me to try it myself, but I thought it would be too embarrassing. When I finally worked up the nerve to try it, I was amazed at how many other people were doing it, too. It's like waking up early to catch a flight and discovering that the world is bustling at 4:30 A.M. when you just assumed that everyone would be sleeping. If you think it's only for oddballs or losers, think again. If you're at all curious, try it!"

$\mathcal{H}$MMM . . . THE GUY IN THE NEXT CUBICLE IS CUTE

"I have worked with this guy for about a year. I really like him, and I sometimes get the feeling that he likes me, too. How can I find out without having to ask him? I would be afraid that he doesn't feel the same and I would feel like a fool." —S.G.

"*L*ook at your work situation first—is one of you superior to the other on the org chart? Then ask yourself, 'Am I really attracted to this person, or is it the danger factor that's attracting me?'"

"*I* met my husband because we were part of a group of coworkers that socialized with each other. Then we just kept doing silly little things together, just the two of us. I don't think we knew we were actually dating at the time. Finally, it dawned on me that I was attracted to him, and when I told him, he felt the same way. We have been together ever since. Not only did we get married, we're about to be parents."

"If you don't flaunt the relationship—and don't fan office gossip by being too cloak-and-dagger about it—you'll find that most people will be fine with it. Set some boundaries to keep things professional in the office (obviously, no affection in the office), and try not to talk about work all the time. I took the risk because I could tell the guy was special, and it paid off. In fact, we are getting married next year!"

"Go for it—but only if you really think you have a future with this person, and are aware of the risks involved. The more closely you work together, the more sure you should be that this is Mr. Right before pursuing a relationship."

"I believe that any relationship with someone who could be construed as your boss is a bad idea. First of all, it is potentially dangerous for you if it turns out bad. You could put the company at risk. You could get yourself in trouble. You could get him in trouble. The relationship must remain professional if you're his subordinate."

$\mathcal{F}$ROM FRIENDS TO LOVERS: WORTH THE RISK?

"I have developed a crush on a friend of mine. I don't know how to make a transition from platonic to romantic with him. Is it worth the risk of losing a friend?" —R.B.

"*F*ind ways to ask him out casually. If you know he likes a particular band or movie, invite him to go. You don't have to ask him for a romantic night out, just an outing to see what your chemistry is like when the two of you are out alone together."

"*J*ust talk to him about whether there possibly could be something further between the two of you. If you aren't good enough friends to do that, then sex shouldn't even enter the picture."

"The best relationships start out as friends. But just being friends doesn't mean there's relationship potential, either. Before you make a move, be sure that you're not interested in him just because 'he's there,' because that's not a good reason to jeopardize a friendship. If you feel true passion for him, it's worth the risk."

"Be aware that if things don't work out, you'll probably have to take a break from each other before you are able to be platonic friends again. However, if you have a good friendship to begin with, you should be able to recapture it down the road."

"*I* was in a very similar situation, and I ended up marrying him. I have a wonderful marriage now. I think if we hadn't gotten together we would've lost the friendship. As my husband and I have discussed, once we realized there was an attraction there, it would not have been fair to have relationships with others when there was an unexplored sexual and emotional attraction between us. In my biased opinion, I say go for it."

CHAPTER 3

The Ins and Outs of Dating

〜

"Getting to know someone is an investment in time, one that many of us are not willing to make unless we feel the initial meeting is picture-perfect. Be open-minded, and realize that finding a good relationship will take a certain amount of work."

$\mathscr{P}$RE-DATE PREP

"I've got a date coming up. I am so nervous. What can I do to calm myself?" —O.F.

"For dates I am particularly excited about, I shop that day for a fun new outfit. I generally end up wearing something else that I feel more comfortable in, but the shopping helps cool my nerves."

"Go to the gym beforehand. Don't kill yourself—just a small workout to boost your energy and give you that post-exercise glow."

"*I* avoid talking to my mom before I have a date. All her questions—like 'Is he the one?' and 'When will your dad and I meet him?'—just make me nervous."

"*I* always go online to check out where we are going to dinner and get a preview of the menu. It helps to get a feel for how fancy the place is so you'll know better how to dress."

"*B*efore each first date, I tell myself that I am just going to meet someone nice. If we match, that's great. But if we don't, I am still going to have a good time. It calms me down to go in with few expectations."

Getting to Know Him (in Two Hours or Less)

"Can you really get to know someone in just one date?" —*F.D.*

"*B*e interested in what he has to say, encourage him to talk, but also open up a bit. Use little bits of personal information to get closer to him and establish a nice environment in which he can relate to you. Sharing a small personal memory shows that you trust him and are inviting him to share something."

"*D*on't try too hard. I usually break the ice by saying something silly, such as something about being nervous. Or if I'm eating salad I give him permission to tell me if I have something in my teeth. Just keep it lighthearted."

"This first meeting is just so you can make sure there's interest on both sides. Spend the 45 minutes or so chatting about your interests and mutual friends. Make small talk. This isn't the time to get into heavy philosophical discussions, past relationships, or what you're looking for in a relationship. You're just trying to decide if this is someone whose company you enjoy. Have no expectations."

"*Y*ou have to remember to listen. So much is revealed in those early meetings, but we let most of it go over our heads because we're concentrating on how we're projecting ourselves. Pay attention because bad dating scenarios often have red flags all over them from the get-go."

"*L*et go of your expectations of meeting Mr. Perfect and enjoy your dates instead of stressing out about them. Think of it as an adventure, and don't put too much pressure on yourself to launch a new romance."

THE KISS

*"I just had a date that went really well. We had
dinner, got drinks, and he walked me home. But
when we got to my door—no kiss. I've always
thought you are supposed to end a good date with a
kiss. Am I wrong?"* —M.C.

"I dated a guy once who waited four dates to kiss girls he really liked to make it more special. If you don't get a kiss, he may be old-fashioned. Or he may really like you and he's waiting so it will be special."

"At some point in the date, decide whether or not you're interested in kissing him. That way, when the end of the night comes, you'll know what you want to happen and you'll be able to make the circumstances such that what you want is more likely to occur."

"Go with each date on a case-by-case basis and do what feels right to you. Some men will wait and some will try."

"There is no hard-and-fast rule about kissing on the first date. There's nothing wrong with a kiss (if you'd like to go out again), but there's no guarantee that it will happen, either."

"Many men have said to me that they thought I wasn't interested after our first date because I walked away so quickly or only shook their hand. To make it light and easy, I suggest saying, 'I had fun meeting you. If you want to do it again, you have my email address.' That way it's nonthreatening but encouraging, and you don't have to worry about kissing on the first date."

*F*IGURING OUT WHO CALLS WHOM— AND WHEN

"I had a first date last night that I really enjoyed. I would like to see him again but don't know how to take things from here." —K.K.

"*O*ne post-date call to say thank you is perfectly
appropriate. After that, play it by ear. If he's interested
in another date, you'll hear from him. If you don't, that's
pretty much your answer. "

"*I*t's okay to call once, but not twice in a row. The same
goes for emails. I've run this rule of thumb by my guy
friends and they say it's absolutely true. "

"*W*ait until he's at work and leave him a message on his home phone: 'I just wanted to thank you for our date and to tell you I had a really good time. I hope we can do it again sometime soon.' That should open all the doors for him if he's interested in seeing you again."

"*O*nce I'm past the beginning of a relationship—the first few weeks or so—I call as often as I feel like it or have something to say. It could be once a day or once a week."

"*E*very guy I date has the same complaint: 'Why don't you ever call me?' Men expect us to put in some effort. If you really like him and he isn't calling regularly and asking for dates, try being a little more aggressive before you give up."

THE EX FACTOR

"I have been dating a guy for three months, but I don't know anything about his dating history, and he doesn't know anything about mine. How do you bring up this subject? Do I even need to?" —P.L.

"The only thing you each need to know about the other's past is whether you were both practicing safe sex before you met. Numbers and details are really none of your business, nor his."

"If you get the feeling he's carrying a torch for an ex, then keep your distance. That doesn't mean you can't see him at all. Just be cautious when you do. Watch and listen before you invest your heart and time and body in the relationship."

"Never give blow-by-blow details of your relationship history, or numbers. If a guy is very concerned about your past, finding out that you have a history is going to bother him."

"I don't mind talking about my past. If someone asks me about my ex, I talk respectfully about him but don't go into any details. I am honest and brief about it."

"*D*o you think he has feelings for his ex? Suggest that all of you hang out together. If you get to know her, it will make you feel better. If there is truly nothing there but friendship, he won't have a problem with the two of you meeting."

GIVING GIFTS THAT DON'T SCREAM "MARRY ME!"

"I've been dating this guy for about six months, and his birthday is coming up next week. What might be an appropriate gift? I want to imply that I think he's great and I'm looking forward to getting to know him better, not that I want him to be the father of my children." —N.R.

"Get tickets to his favorite sports team, even if they are in the nosebleed section. The gift shows that you know what he likes and that you want to spend time with him doing what he likes."

"If he has a hobby, something small, cheap, and practical is good, such as a couple of golf balls or a few fishing flies. Do *not* get him a new golf club or a set of waders."

"Gift certificates from a record store or a book-
store are a lot of fun. I know it's not very personal,
but sometimes guys just dig that you know what
they like. They don't necessarily want deep
meaning behind it, like we women often do."

"*A*void clothing at this point. It's too personal — and announces, 'I'm your girlfriend!'"

"*G*ood birthday gifts in the beginning of a relationship are small, inexpensive, and nonromantic. Don't spend a whole day trekking all over to find him the 'perfect' gift. Keep it simple, like a CD, a book, or tickets to a concert."

*T*HE RIGHT TIME TO SLEEP TOGETHER

*"I've never waited before having sex in a relationship.
Unfortunately, this has always backfired. How do
you know when it's time?" —R.W.*

"*Y*ou are never going to think, *Gee, I wish we had done it one month sooner.* But there is a really big chance that if it doesn't work out, you might think, *I wish we hadn't done it right away.*"

"*A*s long as you won't regret it, it really doesn't matter when you sleep together for the first time. Just realize the consequences and be safe—your relationship may change, and sleeping together opens you up to the potential of STDs or pregnancy."

"*If* you have any doubts, don't do it. That's your head saying, *Maybe this isn't right.* Give yourself some time to make the decision."

"*Think* about it very carefully, with your brain, not with your emotions or your loins. This is a very important decision. While it might be fun and the sex may even be great, sex changes a relationship. You can never tell beforehand exactly what the changes will be."

"*I* had sex with my fiancé on our first date. When we met, I never thought it would last. Nevertheless, we fell in love. Yes, he respects me, despite the fact that I slept with him on the first date. He loves me despite—even because of—my sexual openness and lack of repression. So having sex early on doesn't have to be the kiss of death."

CHAPTER 4

Getting Rid of Mr. Wrong

⌐

"*D*ating is a process in which we look for someone who's right for us. That means someone who meets our wants and needs as they are. Someone with whom we can be happy and content. Not someone who leaves us frustrated, anxious, confused, and sad all the time. If you find yourself struggling and unhappy, then move on. "

Signs It Should Be the Last Date

"Everyone always talks about the 'signs' being there from the beginning. Well, what are some signs?" —V.L.

"*I* recently set up a blind date with a guy who described himself as five-foot-eleven with brown hair. I was shocked and disappointed when a bald guy who was barely five-foot-seven came over and introduced himself to me. I learned that I need a guy to be honest from the beginning."

"*A* big deal-breaker for me is when he spends the entire time talking about himself and doesn't realize that I am the one keeping the conversation going by asking him questions. This happens often. And when it does, I think to myself, *Never mind.*"

"*O*ne thing that deeply offends my old-fashioned
sensibilities is when my date doesn't get out of the
car to walk me to the door. A guy I'd had a crush
on for years finally took me out for dinner and
a movie. It was going fine until we got to my
driveway. He pulled up to the very end of my
driveway, stared at me until I got out of the car,
and was gone before I got to the door. Needless to
say, I didn't say yes to a second date."

"*If* there is any cursing, rudeness, inordinate anger, or overwhelming negativity, it is a definite no."

"*If* a guy doesn't walk me out of the restaurant and see me to a cab, there probably won't be another date. I've given another chance to two guys who didn't, and they turned out to be duds. In hindsight, I realized I should have known when they just sat there as I was leaving the restaurant."

WHEN HE CAN'T — OR WON'T — COMMIT

*"I have been dating a guy for almost five months
now. He is everything I have looked for, but he
has told me repeatedly that he is not looking for
something serious. I really like him and would like
to keep seeing him, but this is breaking my heart.
How patient should I be?"* —N.T.

"If you have strong feelings for him, give him space but keep yourself available to other opportunities. In these scenarios, only time will tell."

"Don't put your hopes on a man's fear of commitment changing overnight. Decide if you are willing to accept being part of his life on his terms. If you are, prepare yourself for whatever happens. He has made it clear that he makes no promises, so consider yourself warned."

"*If* you are exactly what he's looking for, he should have no problem getting into something serious with you. A guy who meets a woman he is sure is right for him doesn't hold her at arm's length. You can wait it out and hope his feelings change, but there is no guarantee that they will. Or you can move on to find a great guy who does want to be with you without hesitations."

"*A* man may say one thing, but his actions tell you how he really feels. The only thing you can do is decide if his actions indicate that he is the type of boyfriend worth waiting for. If not, then don't hang on too long, expecting something that he's not going to deliver."

"*D*on't wait around for him to get his act together. Go merrily along your way. Get some hobbies, get active, spend time with friends, and—most important—date other men. Many times when a man figures out that a woman doesn't need him to be her everything, he will become more interested."

THE LOWDOWN ON CHEATING

"I just broke up with my boyfriend. I caught him cheating with his ex. He keeps leaving messages, trying to get me back. Part of me wants to move on, but part of me wants to keep trying. Am I being stupid?" —L.H.

"*D*on't settle when there are plenty of men out there that would be loyal to you and make you feel great. To help get you started, check out books by John Gray and Barbara DeAngelis. They can really lend great insight into why you choose the partners you choose."

"*I* decided to give my relationship another try after my boyfriend cheated on me. It was a mess. I found myself getting jealous; I just didn't trust him anymore. So I broke up with him for good. Anyone who catches her boyfriend cheating has to do the same: Step back and be nice to yourself."

"Is there anything in your life history of significant
males treating their women disrespectfully or cheating?
It could be your father, your uncle, your brother. Any
history of women accepting relationships that involved
cheating? If this resonates, talk with a therapist. You
don't have to repeat this pattern."

"I think you'll feel much better if you make up your
mind once and for all: Stay or go. Either you stay and
live with his lies and your suspicion, or leave to tough it
out and eventually find peace of mind. Personally, I'd go;
if someone thinks so little of me as to cheat on me, then I
don't need him."

"It's hard to have an honest, open relationship with someone you don't trust. But, if you feel that you really want to be with this person, and you want to be able to trust him, you should go to couples counseling. You need a chance to vent your feelings and have him listen to you without interruption, and you need to give him the same chance."

*W*HEN THINGS GO FROM BAD TO WORSE

"My boyfriend of one year is suddenly criticizing everything I do. He is very difficult to please. When I try to call his attention to what he's doing, we end up fighting. He says if I'm not happy with things, then that's my problem. I'm beginning to wonder if I should leave. What should I do?" —M.T.

"*E*motionally or physically abusive men rarely change on their own accord. They just become more and more controlling. If you are really committed, you need to try couples counseling with a therapist. If he won't go, it's time to move on."

"*Y*ou have to make a decision. Do you want to continue the way things are, or do you want to make a life for yourself—a life you can enjoy, that you can feel proud of? A significant other should make you feel good about yourself, should celebrate every little thing about you, not put you down in every way. You have to choose what you want."

"*I* had a boyfriend who would blame me for everything. He would make big scenes and scream and yell at me over the most ridiculous things. I finally told him if he ever talked to me like that again, I was gone. He was much more careful after that, but eventually it happened again. I was packed and on the road within 48 hours. I came to realize that I was in an abusive situation and I had to get out. I felt such relief at being away from him, it was incredible."

"One of the problems with abuse—whether it's physical or verbal or emotional—is that after a short time it begins to feel normal. Your self-esteem is shattered and your confidence bottoms out. You lose direction and motivation. Life is too short to head down that road. Take care of yourself first."

"Why are you letting this guy treat you like a doormat? What more can he get away with? You are not his mother. You are not responsible for him, and you are in fact endangering him by enabling him. If you feel you love him, then practice tough love and leave. An abusive man's issues are way too big for you to take on, and it's not your job to save him."

*D*ON'T GO CHANGING TO TRY AND PLEASE HIM

"One of my biggest fears about relationships is that I'm going to have to change myself somehow. I look at my girlfriends in serious relationships, and some of them seem so different to me now. How can I tell if I'm improving myself or losing myself for the sake of a guy?" —K.H.

"*Y*ou can certainly make changes if there are things about yourself you would like to improve. For example, you can strive to lose weight, exercise more, smile more, control your anger, eat more vegetables, get over your fear of intimacy, whatever your issue is. But never change yourself unless you want to—don't lose weight because a guy called you chubby. It has to start with your own sincere desire to change."

"Give some thought to what you are willing to change. What would you refuse to change to accommodate another? What might you give up for the right person? If you have a road map, you are less likely to get lost."

"If you change only to please someone else, you are only denying him and yourself the experience of loving the one-of-a-kind you. Compromise is important, but changing who you are deep down inside is going too far."

"When you become someone you dislike, disapprove of, or don't recognize as a result of a relationship, get out. You've got to think of yourself first."

"The only things about yourself that you need to worry about changing are the things that might stand in your way of a healthy relationship with a good man, such as a fear of commitment, or an inability to communicate your emotional needs. In these cases, change is definitely a good thing and worth pursuing."

CHAPTER 5

Beyond the Two of You

"I introduced my boyfriend to my parents after dating him for about nine months. The next day, my father called me up to tell me how pleased he was that I'd finally found someone I was 'compatible with.' My boyfriend was sitting there when I got the call, and after I hung up with my dad, I told him that I'd have to break up with him, since he was the first guy my father had ever liked. I was only joking, of course. We've now been married for six years."

$\mathcal{I}$NTRODUCING HIM TO YOUR FRIENDS

"I've been dating a guy for a while, and my friends are nagging me to let them meet him. But I'm worried it's going to be weird and awkward." —E.M.

"Your friends should want you to be happy above all else. You need your friends to be a part of your life to make any relationship complete. Introduce them all to this wonderful man, and be sure to include him in your relationships with your friends. Show them all how happy he has made you and allow them to share in it."

"If your relationship is very new and you really feel nervous about introducing him to your friends, wait a little while until you are more secure in the relationship. Then have an informal get-together at your place so that the pressure is off."

"The best way to introduce your boyfriend is at an informal gathering. A bar or restaurant is best, preferably one where you and he have already gone together and feel comfortable. The new guy usually gets a favorable response in this environment."

"Set up a situation where you guys are just 'passing through.' Show up with him somewhere where your friends will be and introduce him. Then say you've got to run. Later, you can ask your friends what they thought of him."

"The best way to engineer a successful introduction is to have a buffer for both your friends and your guy. Have your friends meet after work at a bar with activities—such as darts, pool, or pinball—so there is a distraction in case conversations aren't sprouting up naturally."

DEALING WITH FRIENDS' JEALOUSY

"When I was single, my friends had my undivided attention. Now that I want to spend time with a man, I am having a hard time balancing my time. How can I stay close to them while still spending time with my boyfriend?" —L.T.

"If all you have going on in your life is your boyfriend, and he is all you want to talk about, your friends will get bored after a while, whether they are single or not. Make sure you still have a life apart from him—your career, volunteer work, and hobbies. Do those things without him sometimes, and you will have tons to talk about with your friends other than men."

"I believe that people in healthy relationships make it a point to make plans separately. If the relationship is strong, you don't make these plans because you need space, but because you are pursuing activities and friendships that are important to you and that you enjoy."

"Talk to your friends. Make sure they know that you love them and love to spend time with them, and that you have someone else who is special in your life now. They have to understand that you were bound to meet someone you wanted to spend time with eventually. Try to spend some time with all of you together—either go out to dinner or host a dinner party to get the ball rolling."

"*H*aving independent lives within the container of a relationship is healthy. No matter how close you are, you can never fully share your different worlds. You need to find an amount of separateness that will work for both of you."

"*W*hen a relationship is new, a couple usually wants to spend a lot of time alone together. But if one or the other starts cutting off their friends totally, or gives up activities they really loved to do previously, something is wrong. If you're feeling like you need to come up for air, do it."

Meeting Your Parents

"I'd like to introduce the man I've been dating to my parents without making too big a deal out of it. Any advice?" —E.L.

"*I*nvite your parents and your man out to dinner. Meet at the restaurant, have a nice meal, talk about small things, and make sure you pay since you asked them out. This way your parents don't have the home-court advantage."

"*W*ait until you really know him well. Think about how uncomfortable it would be for him to be thrown in with your family on top of not really knowing you. I don't invite men to family functions unless I am serious about them. If I'm just casually dating someone, I would rather be with my family alone than have some guy there I have to entertain."

"Invite him over to your parents' house casually by saying something like 'You're welcome to stop by the barbecue.' But avoid anything that sounds like 'It's time to meet my family because you're the one.'"

"Think of something he does well—whether he's a barbeque king, an expert fly fisherman, or great with kids. Then try to incorporate that talent into the event so that he has a chance to look competent and charming. He will have something to distract him from all the pressure, and he can relax and be himself."

"Be considerate of your man in this situation—
he'll be trying to negotiate your family dynamic,
which has been set for years, so he's the visiting
team. Give him a leg up by having the meeting at
your apartment or somewhere else where he's
comfortable. Think about it: Would you rather
meet his parents at their house, or somewhere
where you feel more at home? Offer him the same
consideration."

STARTING OFF RIGHT WITH HIS FAMILY

"I've been dating a guy I really like for about two months. He's going to a family event soon, and I'm hoping he'll invite me. How can I get him to take me along—and how do I make a good impression if he does?" —S.R.

"Some people are actually embarrassed by their family—maybe they're from the wrong side of the tracks or maybe one of the family members acts funny. If he waits longer to introduce you to his family than you expect, it may not have anything to do with you."

"Don't be too clingy with your man. That's a sure way to turn his parents off."

"No matter what happens, be open-minded.
Judging someone by his family's behavior is not
really fair. Who doesn't have dysfunctional people
in their family? I am nothing like either of my
parents and certainly wouldn't want their mistakes
held against me."

"*If* a guy you like wants you to meet his family, it's a good sign that he feels strongly about you, but try not to overanalyze or read too much into it. If you want to know how he feels, just ask him."

"*Don't* be shy. They'll probably ask you a million questions, so just answer them in a way that fosters conversation—not just 'yes' or 'no.' And if you really want to seal the deal, offer to help out with dinner or to help clean up."

CHAPTER 6

From Mr. Maybe to Mr. Right

"Don't ask yourself, 'Does he like me? Does he view me as his girlfriend?' Instead, ask yourself, 'Do I like him and view him as my boyfriend?' You can't take responsibility for what he wants, but you can take responsibility for making your wants and needs known."

So YOU THINK YOU'VE FALLEN FOR HIM

"How do you know you're in love? And if you are, how can you tell if you have the lasting kind of love?" —H.P.

"Being 'in love' in the early stages often involves getting excited before seeing him, having butterflies, not being able to sleep, daydreaming about him, wanting to be with him all the time. This stage does not last forever. It will either fade altogether, or transform into a strong bond that includes a willingness to give, protect, and sacrifice for the other person."

"You need to see how he acts in different situations: in times of stress, interacting with family, relating to friends. You need to give yourself the time to get to know the person and genuinely like him in addition to loving him."

"It is so important to get to know each other really well before you decide he is the man of your dreams. Are you sure he will not let you down when you need him the most? Is he understanding? Will he accept you and love you just the way you are, or will he criticize you? It's a good idea to write down any questions like these, questions that make you think."

"The older I get and the more relationships I have, the more firmly I believe that love takes time. I just don't believe true love can evolve without knowing someone, being friends with them, learning about them and with them, and growing together over many, many months, or even years."

"There is no set definition anyone can give you about what it means to be 'in love.' I could tell you what I feel like when I'm in love, but it would probably be different for every other woman I know. It's a unique experience for everyone. What matters is how you feel about each other and how you treat each other. Just enjoy what you're feeling and don't get preoccupied with labels—what you're experiencing will be the same no matter what you decide to call it!"

FIGURING OUT WHERE YOU STAND

"When is it a good time to ask a guy where you stand? And what exactly do you ask so you don't freak him out or make him think that you're pushing for more?" —A.G.

"In the first few months of a relationship, don't worry about setting the parameters. Know that you are experiencing these times with him and enjoy how special they are. Don't worry about the future or make unfounded decisions about what that future is going to look like. Give yourself room to change your mind as you continue to grow and change as a person."

"Before you initiate any talks to find out where you stand with each other, be clear about how you feel about this guy and what you'd like out of the relationship. It can be scary to initiate such an emotional conversation — all the more reason to have your head straight about what's important to you. If you know what you want, you're more likely to get it."

"*I* dated a guy who told me all the time how much he loved me while he was sleeping with someone else. The guy I'm currently dating has told me exactly once. But he didn't even need to tell me, because I already knew by the way he treated me and the way he acted when he was around me. I think that when a man loves you, you know. Actually saying it becomes icing on the cake."

"*S*o many women think that sleeping with a man or spending the night at his place makes him their man. He isn't your man until he tells you he is your man and there is no one else. And if he says it while you're 'getting busy,' that doesn't count."

"*I* have been dating a great guy for two months. We haven't talked much yet about how we feel for each other. I don't want to put pressure on our situation since we are having so much fun. I've decided to wait until we get to know each other better over time. I'm spending time with friends and alone and casually dating other guys. My time with other people has been giving me enough confidence to tell this guy what I want and feel when the time is right."

$\mathcal{D}$ON'T CONFUSE MR. PERFECT WITH MR. RIGHT

"This guy I've been dating is so sweet and very attractive, but he has some traits I never imagined a boyfriend of mine would have. How do you accept those things about a man that aren't exactly what you hoped to find? Can you try to change those traits?" —S.J.

"*A* very old and wise woman gave me the best advice ever about relationships: 'No one is going to be your perfect match. Whether or not it works is based on whether you are willing to accept the other person as he is.'"

~

"*You* have to be willing to compromise and communicate. If you are willing to talk openly about what bothers you or what you might want him to change, and are willing to listen to what he might have to say about you, you will see marked changes in your relationship."

"It's less about trying to change someone than it is about knowing what you want out of a relationship and then asking for it. Can you make a man more romantic? No. But if he's not as romantic as you want him to be, you can talk to him about it and tell him that you're not happy. You should be with someone who mostly gives you what you need. If you always have to battle him to get what you need, move on."

"It's dangerous to want to change a guy you've just started dating. If you're focusing on things that are wrong with him, you are probably setting yourself up for disappointment."

"We are only human, and this means we all have little quirks. Would your boyfriend really be the same person you fell in love with if he didn't have his particular quirks? My guy drives me crazy sometimes, but it makes me appreciate and love him even more. Just love him for who he is."

$\mathcal{U}$SING THE "L" WORD

*"I have been dating a wonderful guy. My dilemma
is whether or not to tell him that I love him. I
want to tell him how I feel, but I don't want to
make things weird." —I.L.*

"*D*on't say 'I love you' with the hopes of hearing it in return. If you want to know how he really feels about you, look at how he treats you and how you feel when you are with him. Words can be said without meaning at any time. Do you feel loved when you are with him? That is all that matters. If you don't push the issue, the words will come when he is ready and when they have actual meaning."

"*I*f you really want to tell someone you love him, you should. I've been the first to say it in a couple of relationships and have never regretted it. Why hide your feelings? Maybe telling him will start a dialogue about how he feels about you."

"*I* was nervous about telling my boyfriend I loved him. I just had this idea in my head that he should say it first. Then September 11 happened, and I realized that our relationships are the most valuable things we have and that we need to tell the people we care about how we feel about them. So I said it. And I felt so much better, it wouldn't even have mattered if he hadn't said it back. (He did.) Don't let a preconceived notion that the man should go first hold you back from telling him how you feel about him."

"*I*'ve learned that life is too short to keep my romantic feelings hidden, and to feel secure enough about myself to share my affection. I am realizing that the key to knowing when to say 'I love you' is feeling secure with who you are independently and in your relationship."

"*B*ottom line: Love is a risk. Every time you put yourself out there and make yourself vulnerable, you might get hurt. That's how it works. It's not easy, but when you find someone who feels the same way you do, it's worth it. Just remember that you probably will never find the pot of gold if you don't risk stepping out to look for it."